Max Your Talents Despite All Odds

Gary Calhoun

Max Your Talents despite all odds
Copyright © 2017 Gary Calhoun
Kindle Edition
No portion of this book may be reproduced, scanned, or
distributed in print or electronic form without permission.
Printed in the United States of America
First Printed, 2017
Join With Destiny Publishing
Cover Design by Join With Destiny Publishing
Editing by Mari Brown
Formatting by Sheila Rivera
ISBN-13: 978-0-692-85398-6
ISBN-10: 0-692-85398-7
Library of Congress Control Number: 2017903211

To my wife, Leisa
I love you! Thank you for your love, for believing, for trusting, and for being supportive. You are such a kind, sweet and caring person, which makes you even more beautiful. Never change! You are definitely the love of my life!

To my son, William
I love you. You are a wonderful son with a big heart. You are witty, respectful and carefully considerate of others. You can accomplish whatever you set your mind to and have a passion for.

To my daughter, Lindsey
I love you. You are beautiful, sweet, kind and quietly reserved. You are a very special person. You are a lovely daughter and will always be my little Angel. Follow your passion.

CONTENTS

The book is dedicated to bringing hope
to people who may feel overwhelmed
by the adversity of life.
It is my desire that it will supersize the
motivation of this group of people that
are hurting and boost their faith,
confidence, and commitment to the
level that will cause them to change the
direction of their life

ACKNOWLEDGMENT

I want to give a big thanks to all the people that I have been blessed to meet throughout my life. Even though I couldn't even begin to name them all, I want to give thanks to everyone that has made an impact on me.

I want to give a special thanks to my Mom, Lucille, and my Dad, Allen (deceased) for their steadfast love and support. I am beyond blessed by having them as my parents. There simply could be no one better. They offered unconditional love and continual support, even when I was going in a direction totally opposite as to the way they had raised me to go.

I also want to thank Uncle Bobby and Aunt Martha Jo Calhoun for simply being the epitome of outstanding kin people. Many of my fondest childhood memories include them, along with my cousins, Greg and Anita.

I also want to thank my dearest friends Chuck and Sandy Norton, David and Beverly Mayo, Marty and Ruth Moore for their unfailing friendship of over 26 years, who have been an inspiration and a continual source of input and support. I also want to thank my friends Papa Don and Mama Gail Schroeder, Gary Watson, Rev. Wes Alvarez, Keith Tobias, Donna Alvarez, John Newlin, and many others that I may have failed to mention. I LOVE and deeply appreciate all of YOU!

I also want to thank the following ministers and authors that have validated much of the ideas and beliefs I've written about, who include: Jentezen Franklin, Tony Evans, Ron Carpenter, Steven Furtick, TD Jakes, Joel Osteen, Creflo Dollar, Donald Hilliard, Kenneth and Gloria Copeland, Bill and Eric Johnson, John Gray, Joyce Meyers, Josh Lipscomb, Andy Andrews, AW Tozer, Glen Staples, Jack Graham, Evon Horton, James Gills, Len Ballenger, Ronald Nash, Ed Delph, Alan and Paula Heller, David Stein, Greg Rice, Charles Young, Owen Oslin (deceased), Norvel Hayes, and all the ones that I may have unfortunately forgotten. You are all loved and appreciated!

FOREWORD

I know what the person meant by saying, "You never know how strong you are until being strong is your only option." Unfortunately, so does my family because they had to live it right along with me. The chances are that you or someone you love has also gone through devastating things. It happens. If you are having it hard – facing adversity – feeling overloaded – needing answers and direction – and wondering if anybody cares, even God, you're not alone!

Problems are not discriminatory. It doesn't matter your skin color, corporate status, or how financially blessed or devastated you may be. Life can be extremely hard for all people. Since our future is shaped by the decisions we make, reading this book could be time well spent. It brings a different perspective you may not have been aware of or living at the moment!

As you read it, I believe you will become encouraged that something can be done about your situation! To further elevate your faith, I'll take you through some of my personal experiences that confirm what I'm sharing with you is true. Read this book with the absolute certainty that our Heavenly Father made provisions for any bad decisions you have made and is waiting for you to grasp that so He can start guiding you to the next level.

CHAPTER 1
THE BEAR

My Dad started taking me deer hunting when I was 5 years old. We would go early in the morning and be on our stand before daybreak. A hunting camp tale had it that a bear had been killed a few years earlier in the area where we were going to hunt. That morning, Dad had put me on a stand by myself, while he sat a short distance away. My mind was racing with thoughts of the bear and what to do if I saw it. My father seemed miles away as my anxiety soared. A five-year old's perception makes everything larger than life.

After what seemed like an eternity, the sun began peeking through the trees. When it became light enough to see, my eyes immediately focused on something that scared me worse than I can verbalize. Some 30 feet in front of me was what appeared to be a bear! It was behind a tree. First, it would look at me from around the left side of the tree, disappear, then look around the right side.

I don't have the skills to articulate the level of fear and horror I was experiencing. I did the only thing I knew to do. I let out a blood-curdling scream hollering, "Daddy, Daddy, Daddy!" He came running, "What is it, son?" I said, "It's a bear Daddy! He's behind that tree. He's playing peek-a-boo with me." The look on his face of serious concern shifted to a smile as he sat down, pulling me up into his lap and wrapping his arms around me. He said, "Son, bears don't play peek-a-boo with you. There's no bear. You just thought there was."

Zig Ziglar said, "The best acronym for FEAR is False Evidence Appearing Real." Whether the bear was real or not had no effect on the enormous level of panic I was experiencing. While that event was developing, I couldn't on my own recognize that it was nothing more than a manipulative mind trick.

That was a long time ago, and I still remember it as vividly as if it was yesterday. I can also remember sitting in my dad's lap and safely wrapped in his arms, looking at the tree ~ "the place" ~ where I thought with absolute certainty that something of great danger was about to overtake me, only to realize it was my imagination.

When I was safe in the arms of my father, I found comfort, security, and had the ability to look at the situation differently. It's my desire that when you have situations come against you that appear overwhelming and causing intimidating fear, that this information will help you see things differently. Hopefully it will help you understand that your Heavenly Father is waiting to act on your behalf to destroy the manipulative lies of the enemy.

CHAPTER 2
ADVERSITY

Years back my wife and I started having things fall into place and were doing pretty well financially. It appeared I had this financial thing whipped and my years of persistent and consistent efforts to build a big business were paying off. It felt so good. We were riding the mighty high. Then we met with a little adversity. As one of my late friends would say, "Have you had any adversity or are you in the "adversity-free" group?"

My wife and I ran head-on into Goliath and every one of us has had to face our own personal Goliath (big giant that David faced and defeated in the Bible). There's one thing I found out about the big boy. He plays hardball. I've often said if I ever find that uncircumcised Philistine, I'd like to knock his eyes out. Our business that I worked tirelessly to build vaporized overnight. We fell from financial grace. We went from the mountaintop to the valley, hitting every limb and overhang in our descent. We ended up in a place I never wanted to be – broke - busted - disgusted - cars going back to the Credit Union - house going back to the Bank - and my wife and I going back to first base. The only thing we had left was a solid foundation - ROCK Bottom!

I was just at that place in life where it seemed like everything I laid my hand to would wither. It was like the financial overseers were sitting up in the clouds and every time I would approach an opportunity, they would say, "Gary's getting close to it, KILL IT!" The Bible says that I'm responsible for the financial well-being of my home. If I'm not, I'm worse than an infidel. So, I started desperately praying for restoration. When you're praying for restoration, you know that things haven't gone well. When you get in your 50's, you're not supposed to be starting over. You're not meant to be starting over at any age, but it can happen! And when it occurs, no matter what age you are, there are two choices ~ do nothing and stay in that situation, or do something about it. It was during this time that I was shown something that seemed so simple but had an enormous impact in my life.

Now listen - I'm just a marlin-fishing, flounder-gigging, scuba-diving kind of guy that spent many of my growing up years in the great State of Alabama. And YES - our Heavenly Father and I both are big Crimson Tide fans! But here's the point - if the information I was shown helped me, and scores of others, there's no doubt it can help you. But, before I share the specifics, let's find out where you may be!

CHAPTER 3

WISH YOU HAD SOME DO-OVERS?

Think back to when you were young and what you wanted to be when you got to the age you are now.

How well are you doing? A little off track? Wish you had some do-overs? BREAKING NEWS: We all wish we had some do-overs. We all had other plans – other dreams – other thoughts about the way our life was going to be. Now, we wonder what happened. But that's not the end of the song. You haven't finished writing your life song yet.

No matter what your present situation may be, you can achieve what our Heavenly Father planned for you to achieve. However, you may very likely respond to that statement by saying, "Oh, you don't know my situation. You don't know the terrible decisions I've made. You don't know how bad I've blown it. It may work for other people, but it won't work for me!" You may feel that you have made wrong decisions that eliminated your chances to have a good life. You may feel that you've messed up so bad that even our Heavenly Father doesn't care about you anymore and trashed any plans He had for you. You may think He's wondering why He even put you on this earth.

NOTHING IS FURTHER FROM THE TRUTH! Not only can our Heavenly Father use you, He specializes in our group! No matter how bad you think you've blown it, you are an incredible person wonderfully made by our Heavenly Father, the Creator of the universe for a particular purpose. And, He knew you were going to mess up before you messed up!

In his message titled "I am #8," John Gray said, "You may have been marginalized by circumstances. But, there are no illegitimate children. There are illegitimate events, but there are no accidental lives. You can't sneak into the earth. And if you're here, you have a purpose! Whether your father was in your life or not! Whether your mother planned you or not! Whether people wanted you here or not! You are here because God wanted you here. You have a purpose!"

In the Bible, when God spoke, He spoke in Hebrew. It's interesting to find that the word "Coincidence" doesn't even exist in Hebrew because there is never a situation that catches our Heavenly Father off guard! He never says, "Wow, I didn't see that coming," or "That's a surprise." No, He plans and orders your steps and something happening by coincidence never crossed His mind.

Do you think our Heavenly Father would have gone through such meticulous details in designing your existence if His plan would face derailment due to some weakness that caused you to fail? In the Bible, Peter's failures didn't surprise Jesus. He predicted it. He told Peter when he would fall and predicted Peter's return (Luke 22:31-32). Psalms 139:16 (NLT) says,

"You saw me before I was born. Every day of my life was recorded in your book. Every moment was laid out before a single day had passed."

Just as Peter had to live with the consequences of his decisions, so do we! The outcome of our entire life comes down to two things: DECISIONS we make and PASSION in which we pursue them. Everything about you to this point in your life is a decision you made. You decided on the place where you live, the car you drive, the clothes you wear, and the type of cell phone you have. You decided to read this book!

Everything about you up to this moment in your life is the result of the decisions you have made up to this point in your life!

Therefore, is it safe to say that your choices determine your future? ABSOLUTELY!

Look at your life – look at the choices you have made. They equate. In Jonah 1:1-17, God instructed Jonah to go to Nineveh, but he chose not to go. Instead, he got on a ship going the other direction. So, God sent a strong wind that was destroying the ship and Jonah had to "fess" up. It's an interesting story of how Jonah ended up doing what God wanted him to do, but only after making some bad choices.

It's hard for us to "fess" up and admit that we've made some less than perfect decisions. LOL! But, we must own our blunders before we can move forward. The blame game can't be played anymore! We must own it! But, when we make mistakes, it's easy for us to develop the feeling of being weak, worthless, and undervalued.

That may be human nature, but it's not how our Heavenly Father feels.

Just like Gideon felt when God called him to save Israel from the Midianites, he replied that he was the least of the least, but God called him a mighty man of valor (Judges 6:12-15)! It is the same way with you! You are a hundred times the person in His eyes than you are in your own eyes!

"Whether people wanted you here or not, you are here because God wanted you here. You have a purpose!" John Gray

CHAPTER 4

AWESOMENESS OF YOUR CREATION

Before the world was created, our Heavenly Father designed us with a specific Purpose and Destiny (Genesis 2:7 and Jeremiah 1:5). Purpose means what we were born to do and Destiny is the sum of all we were born to accomplish. This was already intact when you were born.

GRASP THESE NEXT THREE PARAGRAPHS!

Everything about you was designed by our Heavenly Father. He says you are fearfully and wonderfully made (Psalms 139:14). He chose your eye color, height, personality, passion, tendencies, desires, even your hair color (Ephesians 1:4, 2:10)! The hairs on your head are numbered, not just counted – numbered. When a hair falls out, He not only knows that it fell out - He knows that it's hair number 9,256 (Matthew 10:30).

He even sets the years and region you live in (Acts 17:26). He could have placed you in any time period and location in the world. You could have lived in Noah's day, King David's day, Abraham Lincoln's day, or the next generation. You could have been a Roman soldier during His crucifixion. He could have put you

18

in Russia, China, or a Third World country. But He chose to put you here in this region at this time. Before your parents were even born, He already had planned the direction for your life!

Have you ever wondered why? It's because His place, plan, and purpose for you was in this timeslot and location! After all, He knows everything about you. He's your manufacturer. He knows your output capability, and He knows what you are specifically designed to do (2 Timothy 1:9). You're not a cookie-cutter creation; you are one-of-a-kind. Not one person out of all the billions of individuals that have lived ~ or are living now ~ or who will ever live ~ has your identity, your DNA, your fingerprint ~ or was put here on earth to do what you were put here to do.

CHAPTER 5

IF I'M SO SPECIAL, WHY IS LIFE SO HARD?

I can visualize you saying... "Well Dadgum, if I'm so important, why in the heck is life so hard?" Because of that very reason! You're important! The failure of the enemy to destroy your life is an indicator of our Heavenly Father's purpose for your life. The enemy knows what you're capable of accomplishing! Remember his previous employment? He was Heaven's worship leader! He was there when our Heavenly Father created you with your purpose and gave you your potential for greatness.

Now let's fast forward to today. Since that time, the enemy got caught up in pride and was kicked out of heaven. He's very aware of the incredible life God planned for you. And - he hates it! He hates you with a passion – and will do everything within his power to destroy you. He hates you for the things you have hidden in you. He's very cunning, and if we are not constantly aware of his tactics, we allow ourselves to make wrong decisions due to his influence on us.

In his book, "After the Fall," Donald Hilliard wrote, "Can you start to understand why the enemy will try to do everything within his power to stop you? You see why the enemy wants you to lose trust in our Heavenly Father, and doubt what He says? Satan knows if he can keep you from truly trusting God, he can keep you bound in loneliness and mediocrity, which will limit you to believe only in your own resources and ability." Donald also continued with this powerful statement, "Recognize with a keen awareness that you have a spiritual predator, who has had thousands of years to study human behavior. He has carefully perfected his collection of baits and hooks for the human soul. He knows every emotional and physical button to push, and he will do anything to subvert you. He follows no rules and has no conscience. Although you shouldn't fear him, you should certainly acknowledge his existence and learn everything you can about his tactics."

II Corithians 11:14-15 (NLT) states, "But I am not surprised! Even Satan disguises himself as an angel of light. 15 So it is no wonder that his servants also disguise themselves as servants of righteousness. In the end, they will get the punishment their wicked deeds deserve." 2 Corinthians 2:11 (NLT) states, "so that Satan will not outsmart us. For we are familiar with his evil schemes." The only reason you're alive today is because of the love and protection of our Heavenly Father and whatever His plan was for you is still His plan for you. He made provisions for your bad decisions.

Our Heavenly Father desires that no one is lost. He wants everyone to know the love of His Son, Jesus

Christ. He chose to work through us to win others by showing love to our family, neighbors, co-workers, strangers, and friends. Each one of us has a vital individual part to play. If we discover and pursue our Purpose, His desire is accomplished!

On the other hand, the enemy desires that everyone is lost. He attacks us to destroy our faith and effectiveness. He's had a long time to perfect his attack game. He knows your weaknesses and plays dirty, but he's no match for the power that our Heavenly Father gave us to defeat him.

Whatever God planned, prepared and allocated for you before He laid the foundations of the world – is still available to you. His plan is irrevocable (Romans 11:29). He never gives up on you ~ clear evidence that your present situation does not derail your Destiny. It can only incarcerate it for that period of time that you allow it.

Since our Heavenly Father is the source, there is no shortage of resources. Everything needed for carrying out His initiative is readily available, but there is one thing He is looking for ~ people He can trust! The more faithful you are with what He gives you, the more He pours into you, expanding your resources, and enabling you to pursue your purpose.

II Chronicles 16:9 (NKJV) says, "For the eyes of the Lord run to and fro throughout the whole earth, to show Himself strong on behalf of those whose heart is loyal to Him." It doesn't say He's looking for the perfect "vessels," or "clean" vessels. He's looking for the "available" trusting vessels.

To God, your life is like a canvas that's already painted. He knows the end from the beginning.

He says, "I am the Alpha and the Omega, the First and the Last, the Beginning and the End." Revelation 22:13 (NLT).

Some of you may be going through things that have caused your faith to grow weak. But, if you could see into the future and saw yourself – looking good – feeling good – and smelling good, you wouldn't be stressed. You would know everything was going to be fine. Since you can't see that, you must trust Him. It's not the way we would prefer it, but your faith must start out before you know how it's going to turn out.

God doesn't design faulty plans. He doesn't make mistakes. He doesn't get shocked or surprised. Be assured that God didn't get caught off guard by any perceived failures or actions that created the present circumstances of your life, or that caused you to feel disqualified. Don't misunderstand the reason, necessity, or advantage of your current situation. Don't neutralize your uniqueness!

Man's labels and limitations do not change God, derail God, limit God, or stop God! This is a foundational, fundamental truth that you should lay claim to with such fervor and conviction that it resonates from the very core of your being. It doesn't matter what you've had or what you've lost. What you have now is all you need to start. Do not let what you cannot do interfere with what you can do!

Chapter 6
What If?

One of my favorite stories in the Bible is about Joseph. Part of his story is very much like many of ours. God had some stuff planned for Joseph to go through before he would be ready for his Purpose. So, He put Joseph through an endurance course that would develop him into the person that He could trust.

Joseph endured things that were very painful – he was betrayed – lied about – forgotten – things that you may have experienced. But, in one day – one 24-hour period - he went from prison to the palace, operating beside the most powerful man in the world.

I love what Psalms 105:19 (NLT) says, "Until the time came to fulfill his dreams, the Lord tested Joseph's character."

Have you ever thought that possibly what you're going through could be God testing and building your character for your future position He has purposed for you to do?

CHAPTER 7

YOUR DREAM

What's your dream? Only you know! I do know that you have one because our Heavenly Father gave each of us a dream. Throughout the Bible, we find where people described their dream. Joseph had a dream. That's what seemed to start his trouble. He told his brothers! Joseph's dream was that he would be the leader of a nation and his family would bow down to him, which was totally against the culture. Older never bowed to younger.

Our Heavenly Father gives us dreams because He knew we would need something to keep us motivated and committed. He's given you a dream. You may have thought it was just a crazy idea. If so, you may want to give it more attention because your dream contains your Purpose and everything that will bring joy and the feeling of significance to your life. Also, your dream is your dream! Be careful who you tell. Everybody's not going to respond with your best interest, just like with Joseph's brothers, unfortunately, there's jealousy. If you achieve your dream, it makes them look bad!

HOW DO I FIND MY PURPOSE?

By re-discovering your Dream! Your Dream contains your Purpose ~ your Purpose contains your blessing, which includes your resources that are in direct proportion to your Purpose. Your dream is where your uniqueness becomes evident. It's like a magnet. Your dream draws you toward something like a magnet attracts metal. It's that mental picture you have of where you want to be and what you want to do. It contains your Purpose – your assignment and task, which ultimately leads you to your Destiny – your end results and destination. Your purpose is hidden in your heart so that it won't be corrupted. His plan is to prosper you, to give you a future and a hope (Jeremiah 29:11). His plan includes giving you the desires of your heart! (Psalms 37:4). His plan is to give you life, and life more abundantly (John 10:10).

"If you can't figure out your purpose, figure out your passion for your passion will lead you right into your purpose." T. D. Jakes

DON'T UNDERESTIMATE THE POWER OF THE DREAM

Our Heavenly Father is big into dreams – big dreams! A goal gives you motivation, determination, and direction to achieve what it is you seek. Our Heavenly Father gave each of us an original vision, and to Christians, He gave us a corporate dream, Heaven. He could have just "surprised" us after we passed away. But God knew that we were going to face some adversity and would need a BIG dream of something

27

better than we would ever have here to keep us focused.

Think about Abraham – our Heavenly Father knew there would be times when Abraham would have a hard time believing that he was going to have a son at his age. Therefore, God gave him two great visuals... Stars and Sand! In Genesis 22:17 (NLV), He told Abraham that his descendants would multiply like the stars in the sky and the sand on the seashore. If Abraham should doubt, he could only look up at the sky or look down at the sand and be reminded of God's promise.

CHAPTER 8
YOUR CAPACITY

Lottery winners experience a tremendously happy financial event. However, it's a known fact that seventy percent of the winners wind up bankrupt. According to a 2010 study by researchers at Vanderbilt University, the University of Kentucky and the University of Pittsburgh, the more money you win in the lottery, the more likely you are to end up bankrupt.

Why? They simply aren't prepared to handle it. Being out-of-sync with your self-image is as dangerous as an atom being overloaded with neutrons and having to burst apart. There's no such thing in the universe as a person being out of harmony with their self-image for any measurable period of time. Statistics show that if a rich person wins the lottery, he just becomes richer and experiences little change. If a poor person wins, a high percentage of them become devastated.

Our Heavenly Father operates exceedingly, abundantly above all that we ask or think, which is evidence of that fact that He has something much greater for us than we can grasp at our present level (Ephesians 3:20). To discover it will take nurturing and development. He will not open doors for you prematurely. You've got to be able to handle whatever He has for you because it's designed to be good and not harm. If it's not in the right timing, it can harm you. Therefore, our progression and growth should become a daily activity.

Giving your son or daughter a car at the age of 16 could be a perfect gift and great timing. Giving it to them at the age of six is not. Even though it's the same child, same parent, and same car, it would most likely result in devastation, rather than the intended blessing! "An inheritance obtained too early in life is not a blessing in the end." Proverbs 20:21 (NLT) It's the same with the release of our Heavenly Father's resources to us. The magnitude of our scope and responsibility should match the proportion of His release.

WHAT IS YOUR CAPACITY?

What's the amount that you can handle? Whatever it is, it's personal. Only you know. Think again of the analogy of lottery winners, could most lottery winners handle winning one dollar? Probably, right? So where does their self-image and self-worth separate? At one thousand, a hundred thousand, a million, ten million?

Wherever it happens to you is the limit of your capacity, and our Heavenly Father is not going to pour a blessing into a vessel that is incapable of containing it. In Malachi 3:10, God says He will pour out a blessing so great you won't have enough room to take it in! This proves His blessing is bigger than you could ever contain, meaning you will only get what you can contain. Therefore, the larger we can expand our capacity, the greater the volume of blessing.

It was the same way with the widow's blessing. Her blessing size was determined by the number of vessels she gathered when Elisha instructed her to do so. (2 Kings 4:3-6).

He told her to borrow as many empty vessels as she could and fill every one of them with oil. She did, but when there were no more empty vessels, the oil stopped flowing. Therefore, her blessing was determined, limited, controlled, regulated, reduced, constrained, restricted, hampered, and ultimately ended with only one thing ~ her capacity in the number of vessels she gathered.

Our blessing size is regulated by our capacity.

Our blessing size is regulated the same way – by our capacity. If God has unlimited resources, your possible access to abundance is unlimited! Therefore, mindsets and skill-sets must be nurtured and developed for your ability to increase. When you expand your blessing capacity, you alleviate the only factor restricting your overflow of resources.

The size of your talent and impact of your purpose is immeasurable from the start. God releases His plan for you incrementally. He will never let you see the entire picture because God thinks "exceedingly abundantly above us." (Ephesians 3:20-21).

If He let us see what He had planned for us to accomplish we wouldn't believe it and sure wouldn't have faith to believe we could. We would be just like Moses when God appeared to him in the desert and told him what He wanted Moses to do. Remember what Moses said to God... What? Me? Who am I that I should go? (Exodus 3:11) In his wildest imagination, Moses couldn't believe what God wanted him to do.

We, also, would want to side-step our faith-building process that develops and matures us to handle the task at hand. So, God doesn't let us see everything. Instead, He takes us systematically through faith! As you follow His guidance and apply your talents on an ongoing basis, your ability increases along with your capacity! You could ask any person that is recognized for having reached a tremendous level of service if, in the beginning, they ever dreamed of making the impact they made. They would say no. But, as they were faithful, our Heavenly Father increased their capacity for them to make a larger impact.

The enemy knows this and doesn't want you to come to the realization that accomplishing what you were designed to achieve is literally at your fingertips. When you become motivated to explore your potential, he goes into attack mode and does everything he can to discourage your attempt. He will bring up your past failures and tells you that you're not worthy of it. Sadly, since most of us don't feel entitled or capable, it's an easy battle for the enemy to paralyze our efforts. Unfortunately, most of us count ourselves out before we even try. Why? Our self-image!

YOUR SELF-IMAGE

Everyone of us has this self-image of where we belong in life - of what kind of house we should live in - the car we should drive – and the job we should have. The fact is there's no more truth to it than a man on the moon. Everybody belongs in life exactly where they can picture themselves in life. Power, money, and success don't care who owns it. It's not discriminating whatsoever. It's just there for whoever believes they're entitled to it ~ and whoever believes that - they get it.

Your self-image should be established by actually understanding who you are and what you have! You are a child of the King! There's nobody like you so no one can do what you are to do! Your purpose is too important not to pursue! If you don't feel worthy or capable of it, you won't seek it. If your self-image doesn't match the position you "should be" in, you won't attain it. Everything about your life – your feeling of real accomplishment and true worth ~ access to resources – your blessing - and the capacity to have life effectiveness with tremendous eternal value – is all tied to your purpose.

As you become actively involved in pursuing your purpose, your focus should be on how good you can be personally and not how you compare to others. Talents, abilities, and gifts are personal and are not measured against anyone else. Our Heavenly Father uniquely made each one of us. "For we are each responsible for our own conduct." (Galatians 6:5)

Example: Let's say that you have the ability or capacity to fill a gallon and everyone around you has the capability to fill a pint. If you fill a quart – which is twice as good as everyone else – you will still feel that you didn't accomplish your best because you know that you're capable of filling a gallon.

Don't compare yourself to anyone else. You are uniquely designed by our Heavenly Father. There's no one in the world like you! No one has your DNA, fingerprint, or God's plan (purpose) for your life! (Psalms 139:14). Don't try to be like someone else. You are an original. Don't die a cheap copy of somebody else! If our Heavenly Father had wanted Billy, He would have made Billy. If He wanted Susie, He would have made Susie. He made you because He wants you!

Galatians 5:26 (MSG), "Since this is the kind of life we have chosen, the life of the Spirit, let us make sure that we do not just hold it as an idea in our heads or a sentiment in our hearts, but work out its implications in every detail of our lives. That means we will not compare ourselves with each other as if one of us were better and another worse. We have far more interesting things to do with our lives. Each of us is an original."

CHAPTER 9

SEEKING AN ANSWER

S o far, we've discussed how you were awesomely created with a dream - that internal vision to guide you to your purpose, along with the talent and available resources to accomplish it. We've also explained about your capacity and self-image, and how important it is to feel entitled to all our Heavenly Father has planned for you. I hope you are starting to feel better about yourself, your future, and fully grasping that no matter what your present situation is, there is another side of your story and you are right where our Heavenly Father knew you would be. And, that He has made full provisions for you to make up for your wrong decisions. But – you must act on your provisions!

MAX MELITZER

Years ago, Max Melitzer was homeless, pushing a shopping cart on the streets of Salt Lake City, Utah, sleeping under freeway overpasses and at a rescue mission. What Max didn't know was he had become a wealthy man. Max had lived, by his own choice, a homeless life for many years. His family loved him and tried to connect with him, but all contacts gradually were rejected. Max's brother died of cancer, but he loved his estranged brother. So, in his will, he stipulated that Max was to receive a hundred thousand dollars from his estate.

It took a private investigator two months to find Max. He told a news agency, "He'll no longer be living on the street... he'll be able to have a normal life... a home, provide for himself and purchase food and clothing." For Max, the gift of a lifetime, a gift of love, was already his, waiting to be received. (Foxnews.com, June 18, 2011)

Sadly, many of us are just like Max. We are loved so much by our Heavenly Father. He has provided all we could ever need, yet we don't know it and therefore don't act on it. Our human struggle for money and meaning is unnecessary when God has already given the gift of a lifetime. Regardless of the dollars we have or the significance we achieve, it's nothing more than a pushcart in the streets compared to all God declares is ours.

Take a moment right now to close your eyes and visualize our Heavenly Father looking at you with a big smile - giving you the thumbs up - nodding His head in affirmative and saying, "Don't dwell on the past. You can do it. I've got faith in you. I love you. Let's roll!"

Chapter 10

First-fruit Is The Activator

Now back when we were going through our period of frustration and adversity. I started talking to our Heavenly Father as I would my best friend or my own earthly Father. I said, "You say you love me and that you have a specific plan for me, but I don't feel that this matches up with my situation.

We were believers actively attending church. We just also happen to be among the multitude of Christians who were having tremendous financial difficulties. We needed help and direction! We had freedom in Christ but were not experiencing the fulfillment of our purpose.

I'm a businessman - not a minister. I point that out because when a minister speaks about money, some people have a tendency to feel that it's for selfish reasons - I get that. But, this section is from my viewpoint and the advantages we received on a "personal" basis.

It was during this period as I was seeking an answer that I heard someone discussing the specific way to unlock and activate the blessing of God. He talked about the principle of first-fruit. He made the statement that no other giving – other than first-fruit –

enabled the blessing of our Heavenly Father and backed it up with scriptures. He illustrated this principle by taking ten dimes - each representing ten percent of a dollar. He said we could give any one of the ten dimes, but there was only one of the dimes that would unlock the blessing ~ the first one.

I found this to be intriguing. I had been paying tithes periodically, but never remember hearing that paying tithes in a particular order would have such a significant difference in the results. But, from our personal experience, giving our Heavenly Father the first ten percent of our financial increase, which I also refer to as "First-dime," was the main ingredient that changed our lives. There is no other giving found in the scriptures that God acted on other than first-fruit. This precedence was established very early with the first family. In Genesis 4:3-7 (NLT): When it was time for the harvest, Cain presented some of his crops as a gift to the Lord. Abel also brought a gift—the best portions of the firstborn lambs from his flock.

The Lord accepted Abel and his gift, but he did not accept Cain and his gift. This made Cain outraged, and he looked dejected. "Why are you so angry?" the Lord asked Cain. "Why do you look so dejected? You will be accepted if you do what is right. But if you refuse to do what is right, then watch out! Sin is crouching at the door, eager to control you. But you must subdue it and be its master. Abel brought the best of the firstborn and was accepted. Cain just brought some of the crops and was rejected. However, the Lord tells him if he does what is right he will be accepted.

Even though we live under grace, not the law, since our Heavenly Father sent His Son (firstborn), Jesus Christ, to earth to be crucified for our sins, it shows very clearly that our Heavenly Father only operates in "Firsts" whether giving or receiving.

Today, some people claim that giving ten percent was under the law and therefore abolished when Christ came. It's true that we're not under the law, we are under Grace, but our Heavenly Father set His precedence regarding ten percent with explicit details and vivid examples. This principle was established and set into precedence 600 years before the law. Abram gave ten percent of all the increase they had from their battle victories to the Priest Melchizedek in 2075 BC. The law came to Moses in 1445 BC. In Genesis 14:20, Abram (name later changed to Abraham) gave Melchizedek ten percent (a tenth) of all the goods he had recovered. This event established the amount.

I heard Randy Alcorn say, "Does God under Grace lower His standards under the Law?"
He went on to say, "If God required the giving of ten percent from the poorest Israelite farmer, then why do we feel that He would require less from us who are living in the richest culture in human history? In essence, you're saying that you believe it would be fine for you under Grace to give less than God called upon much poorer people to give under the Law! And they

40

hadn't seen the atoning work of Christ, and they didn't have the indwelling of the Holy Spirit.

HOW DO YOU MAKE THAT CASE TO THE LORD AT THE
JUDGMENT SEAT?

Let's face it – most of the time we argue to rationalize
our own lack of generosity in giving. The average
Christian gives about two and a half percent of their
income away. So, that would mean that if we're all
Grace-giving, apparently, Grace is about a quarter as
effective, powerful, and transforming as the Law. I
don't believe that's the way it's to be. The examples in
the New Testament – the poor widow who gives
everything - the Macedonian Christians in 2
Corinthians 8 who out of great poverty gave with
overflowing joy and great generosity – not only
according to their means but beyond their means."

My family and I chose ten percent because that's what
He wanted from the beginning and I don't believe He
lowers His standards. The amount you should give is
between you and God, but nowhere has He not
required giving.

It's hard to expect a Blessing from someone you rob!

Malachi 3:8-11 (NCV) says, "Should a person rob
God?" But you are robbing me. You ask, 'How have we
robbed you?' "You have robbed me in your offerings
and the tenth of your crops. So, a curse is on you
because the whole nation has robbed me. Bring to the
storehouse a full tenth of what you earn, so there will
be food in my house. Test me in this," says the Lord
All-Powerful. "I will open the windows of heaven for

you and pour out all the blessings you need. I will stop the insects, so they won't eat your crops. The grapes won't fall from your vines before they are ready to pick," says the Lord All-Powerful.

WHAT DOES THE BLESSING DO? IT BLESSES!

Let's look at an example from the Bible found in 2 Samuel 6:11-12, as to how it blesses. David was moving the Ark of the Lord, which represented the immediate presence of God and contained the blessing of God. The presence of God blessed Obed-Edom's house abundantly. I would imagine that included whatever was needed for a successful life. The household of Obed-Edom came under intensive blessing. He, his family, and everything around him was blessed.

WHY IS FIRST-FRUIT SO IMPORTANT?

I started pondering why is giving to Him first the activator that releases His blessing? When I took an in-depth look, I found that it's simply because it is tangible evidence of our obedience and faithfulness to Him, which is what He's looking for. How can He entrust us with the awesome purpose He has designed for us, along with all the resources, if we operate outside of obedience and faithfulness?

Our Heavenly Father expects and only accepts first-fruits. He explicitly instructed this type of giving throughout the Bible, starting in Genesis 4:3-7, where Cain and Abel brought a gift to our Heavenly Father.

In the back of the book are additional scriptures regarding first-fruit.

CHAPTER 11
WE PUT IT INTO PRACTICE

The concept of first-fruit resonated with my wife and me. Since it made so much sense, we agreed to give first-fruit, not second or give if we had anything left. No matter what we received monetarily, we made the commitment that we were going to give to Him the first ten percent of our gross (not net). We committed not to spend one penny until this was paid, even if we had to go to the church and slide a check in the door. We made sure this was done first without fail. We started the next Sunday – the only problem was that we had no income, therefore – no first-fruit. We would take a blank empty offering envelope and would pray over it.

Our prayer was, "Father whatever you bless us with we commit to give you the first ten percent!" Then, we would walk down and drop the empty envelope in the basket to outwardly demonstrate our commitment to faithfully give Him the first ten percent of whatever He blessed us with before spending a penny of that money.

Father whatever you bless us with, we commit to give you the first ten percent!

As we continued to stay committed, we seemed to just have things falling into place. Business ideas started popping up in conversations, as well as thoughts that I knew I couldn't have come up with. Opportunities began to develop – business offers started to increase – and we began experiencing a drastic increase in our income.

Within a year after we were holding up blank envelopes with nothing more than commitment, we could give thousands in first-fruit tithes and offerings. All the Glory to God! What a feeling! To experience our Heavenly Father's blessing in our lives from the simple obedience to first-fruit was nothing short of amazing. We were so blessed, and it felt wonderful to honor the commitment we had made to Him.

UNMERITED GROWTH - A FRIEND'S REAL LIFE STORY ABOUT FIRST-FRUIT

I have a friend who is very successful in the commercial real estate industry. He had witnessed the transformation in my life firsthand. One day while we were talking about it, I mentioned first-fruit. Now, he had been connected to church for most of his life but had not been taught about first-fruit either. I told him the story of how my wife and I had learned about it and how it had resonated with us. The story intrigued him, and he said he may try it.

A couple of years or so later, we were having lunch when he mentioned being slammed with more business that he could seem to handle. That statement was profound since we were in a down economy and real estate wasn't moving. I asked him what was causing his business to do so well. He told me that he had not advertised more, he had not worked harder to get more listings. He had not done one single thing to increase his business other than starting to give first-fruit after we had initially talked about it. I literally wanted to jump up and yell right in the middle of the restaurant. When you have something that someone says has worked for them to unlock the blessing of the Heavenly Father – and you try it, and it works for you – and you tell someone, and it works for them. That is an incredible feeling!

CHAPTER 12

WHAT DOES FIRST-FRUIT HAVE TO DO WITH MAXIMIZING YOUR TALENT?

You may be thinking that it seems small and insignificant as to how we pay our tithes. You may ask, "Do you really believe our Heavenly Father cares whether we pay our tithes first or last?" I say emphatically YES and here are a few reasons why:

1 He's a Jealous God!~The Bible states throughout that our Heavenly Father is jealous! For I, the Lord your God, am a jealous God.~Exodus 20:5. Exodus 34:14 says that He is so jealous that His name is Jealous!

2 He only operates in first-fruit! ~ Starting in Genesis 4:4, Abel brought firstborn of his flock! In Exodus 23:16, it's first-fruit of what was sown in the fields. The command to return first-fruit continues throughout the Bible. In the New Testament, He gives us His first-fruit –His Son, Jesus Christ!

3 He requires Trust!~By giving to Him
first definitely proves we trust Him!

4 He operates in ways that may seem
odd or insignificant to solving the
situation.~He instructed Naaman to dip
in the Jordan River seven times if he
wanted to be healed of leprosy. He
wasn't healed until he did. (2 Kings
5:14). In Joshua 6:1-21, He instructed
the people to march around the city
seven times without saying a word.
They did it, and the walls of Jericho fell
flat.

These actions certainly do not fit into our strategies for
receiving our healing or game plan for battle victories,
but it's what our Heavenly Father instructed.
Throughout the Bible, He has instructed first-fruit
with no scripture to contradict it.

SO, WHAT DOES PAYING YOUR TITHES FIRST HAVE TO
DO WITH ACTIVATING THE BLESSING IN YOUR LIFE?

I firmly believe it has everything to do with it! We
cannot maximize our talent without operating under
the first-fruit blessing. From my experience, even
though there are other important factors, which are
discussed here in the book, first-fruit is the catalyst to
access our Heavenly Father's blessing! If it's leftovers to
you, it's leftovers to Him, and He doesn't accept
anything but first! Pay Him first is tithing. Pay Him

later is tipping!

It's also essential for its sustaining power during times of adversity. And believe me, there will be adversity. When you become committed to maximizing your talents - and doing the things you're purposed to accomplish - the enemy will attempt to detour you with obstacles and circumstances. Some that may rock you to the core, but the tangible evidence of the first-fruit blessing will help you trust God with unwavering faith during these times. It will help you endure when you're experiencing intimidating fear - and recognize that it's nothing more than a manipulative lie of the enemy. Remember my bear story.

Unfortunately, it's during these times of adversity that most people quit - fail - and forsake their purpose. Instead of maximizing their talents, like the servants with the five and the two talents, they become like the servant with 1 talent (Matthew 25:14-30).
They never attempt to put their talent(s) into action to accomplish God's great purpose for their life - a tremendous tragedy.
Does it make a difference? It did for us! I believe this is why the enemy so vigorously attempts to void our receipt of God's blessing by spreading false propaganda that the church just "wants our money." If we come to the full understanding of how to unlock our blessing, the enemy has a significant problem on his hands.

Our giving is for our blessing, not the church. But, both get blessed in the process.

If we grasp that our giving is for our blessing, not the church, we are on our way to enjoying tremendous success. In Philippians 4:17-18 (NLT), Paul says, "I don't say this because I want a gift from you. Rather, I want you to receive a reward for your kindness. At the moment, I have all I need—and more!"

CHAPTER 13

MY PERSONAL STORY

As a testimony to the fact that what I'm telling you works, let me give you a few more details from my life. As stated earlier, our business exploded. We were growing rapidly. At the end of our first year, we were listed by an industry rating service as the fastest growing network marketing company in America at that time. In the first 24 months, our business grew to 100,000 affiliates nationwide and produced over $30 million in sales, but here's the rest of the story.

With growth comes an enormous amount of exposure within the network marketing industry, which brings with it jealousy, badmouthing, and scrutiny from many sources. Affiliates often migrate from one opportunity to another due to the dynamic income potential and excitement of being among the first to join the "new" opportunity. We had a new idea that had not been previously offered in the network marketing arena, and it was very attractive and grew extremely fast. After a couple of years of massive growth and success, much to our surprise and dismay, law enforcement raided our growing business. They didn't close our business, just stated they were investigating it and told our employees to continue working. But it made it basically impossible to maintain since they had taken our computers, equipment, and money.

Left home successful - came home broke.

I had driven out of our driveway that morning as a very successful businessman and drove back in that evening not able to buy a hamburger. I walked into the house to find my beautiful wife crying. We had lost our income, our vehicles, and it was painfully obvious that we would lose our beautiful home. Through her tears, she asked, "What in the world are we going to do?" I replied, "We're going to trust our Heavenly Father. He said that if we bring in the first-fruit, He will pour out a blessing on us that we could not contain. I don't know how He's going to do it, but I believe He's going to take care of us!" I honestly thought it too!

Did our Heavenly Father cause this to happen to us? Did He build me up just to tear me down?
Was this a "Joseph thing" where He was putting us through some stuff to develop us? Was this part of His plan from the beginning when He created me before He formed the world? Well, as the ole saying goes, "some things are above my pay-grade." Knowing the answer to these questions indeed, fits that category! I don't know why it happened! Only He Knows! One viewpoint could indicate that I chose the wrong vehicle. Pursuing another opportunity could have yielded more preferred results. On the other hand, if I had chosen another path, there's a 99.9% chance you

would not be reading this book right now!

Here's the important point - if it was His plan for me from the beginning, I was right on target and schedule. If it wasn't His plan, then He knew the results of my decisions and had already made provisions. Either way, it all turns out great if we follow Him with child-like trust and faith which is... Easy to say - Hard to do!

CHAPTER 14

OUR HEAVENLY FATHER HAD ALREADY STARTED TO WORK

Despite the apparent adverse situation, we were in, down inside I had a level of confidence that my Heavenly Father had everything under control. And I was right! He had already started before we had experienced the devastation, but we didn't find out until days after.

On Sunday (7-26-12), two days before the raid, during worship, God laid on a person's heart to come over and tell me something. Since we were merely casual acquaintances, he felt uncomfortable doing so and attempted to just brush it off. By the end of service, he said the urge escalated to where he couldn't resist any longer. He had to come tell me. Unfortunately, we'd left the sanctuary. He got my phone number from a mutual friend a couple of days later and tried to call me. By this time, the raid had occurred, and they had taken my cell phone, so we didn't connect. After trying unsuccessfully to reach me, he called our pastor, who sent word through a friend asking me to call him. When we connected, he told me about the church member and that he wanted to meet for breakfast the next morning. By this time, it was seven or eight days after the raid. He said the word given Sunday before the raid on Tuesday was, "Tell Gary I love him, I know what He's going through, I see him, and have no fear!" I broke. I had to leave the table. When I got into the car, I wept uncontrollably! It was simply overwhelming to know that my Heavenly Father was looking out for me and had everything under control! It reminded me and reinforced the fact that our Heavenly Father is sovereign! Everything that occurs in our life has first been approved by Him! A sparrow can't even fall from the sky without Him knowing and approving it. Nothing slips by Him!

As I left the restaurant, I called a friend to share what had happened and how overwhelming it was for me to absorb. He said, "I can believe it. While praying this morning, I asked our Heavenly Father for a word I could give you today, and He laid it on my heart to tell you that He loves you!"

Then our Heavenly Father started providing tangible evidence of His providential care from His blessing. We were moneyless, carless – and soon to be homeless – but I confidently knew that He would provide! And sure enough, a friend showed up and gave me the keys to his truck and said, "Use it as long as you need it." Shortly after, a family member provided a vehicle. The friend who had prayed for a word to give me said that he and his wife had thought about selling their condominium, but our Heavenly Father had laid it on their hearts that we may need a place and if so – it was ours!

We moved in a few days later to a fully-furnished penthouse condominium at one of the most exclusive golf resorts in the area. The first morning we were there, I went out on the patio while having a cup of coffee. I heard mowers cutting the fairways. God had taken us from two acres that I was responsible for to 165 acres of the well-manicured real estate that I wasn't responsible for. I walked out on the front balcony and saw people cleaning the pool that I didn't have to touch.

My son and I started using the putting green. Occasionally, we would get a five-dollar bucket of range balls. One day my son came out with two buckets and said that the golf pro had charged for my bucket, but had given him his bucket – which he continued to do from that point on. While we were on the driving range, we noticed the club was extremely busy and offered to help – at no pay. The golf pro gladly accepted my offer and asked if we would operate the machine that picked up range balls. My son loved it! When we finished, the golf pro introduced us to the pro shop employers and gave us the same privileges as the other golf shop employees, FREE golf!

This was one of the most prestigious and expensive golf courses in Northwest Florida. I would operate the range ball retriever machine before the course opened which took about fifteen minutes – then play with one of the first groups off the tee. I was coming up to our condominium after playing one day when our next-door neighbor came out and asked if I needed any golf balls. He said he didn't play, but in the evenings, he would walk around the golf course for exercise and picked up lost balls. He started providing me with literal boxes of golf balls... an endless supply!

What was so special to me that I really appreciated about this was the golf course was a tight course, and I didn't have the money to buy golf balls to play. So, to me, this eloquently illustrates how our Heavenly Father is involved in even the seemingly insignificant details! If he had not given me the golf balls, I wouldn't have been able to play. I would have been within a one-minute walk to the course and not have been able to enjoy it. We went from the devastation of losing our home to living at one of the most desirable resorts in a fully-furnished penthouse condominium – playing golf every day I wanted to with an unlimited supply of balls!

You think you can out-do our Heavenly Father? No way! He operates at a level exceedingly abundantly above all that we ask or think... (Eph 3:20) There is nothing better than living under the blessing activated by first-fruit! I can't adequately articulate the abundance of favor my family and I have received, which include financial benefits, physical healings, and a tremendous increase in faith, since the time we made the decision of applying the principle of first-fruit.

PROCESSING THE OUTCOME!

Negotiations started between my attorney and the authorities to resolve the situation. They seemed to believe that our business that was two and a half years old and had grown to over 100,000 affiliates nation-wide somehow could be contrary to the state's convoluted pyramid laws.

We vehemently disagreed, but it's hard to financially mount an adequate defense and court fight, estimated in the range of two hundred thousand dollars, with your assets frozen. After several months of negotiations, the result was reached to take a plea and get the majority of my assets returned, but I would have to serve three years' prison time. Talking about a hard pill to swallow – believe me, this one was ENORMOUS, especially after speaking with a high-ranking officer who told me, "I have no doubt that you would win this case. I don't even bet, but I would bet that you would win." But, you can't afford to fight it when you don't have access to your money.

Words from our Heavenly Father in the eight months while negotiations were going on, there were three different occasions where people had a word from the Heavenly Father for my family and me. The first word was the one previously mentioned where God had said He loved me and have no fear.

The second one was to my mother. She was heavily burdened for the care and safety of my family and was praying for God's protection. She attended a church homecoming with some friends in another city. The visiting minister, who did not know her or have any knowledge of anything that was going on, walked up to her toward the end of the service while people were praying and said, "Your children and your grandchildren are going to be ok." Talk about making a grandmother shout, this did!

The third time was two weeks before I was to report in. A lady came up to me during worship and said she felt uncomfortable approaching someone on her own and had asked an usher to go with her. She said she felt that God had given her the following word for me, "You may not understand the path I have chosen for you, but you're walking in my footsteps now and not your own. I have plans to prosper you and not harm you. Trust me only on your journey." Now, talk about making me shout and feel humbled at the same time, before her walking up I had just prayed basically the same statements to our Heavenly Father.

After seeing how our Heavenly Father was taking care of our every need and having words spoken over the situation three different times, I felt totally at ease that not only was our Heavenly Father taking care of us but that He was weaving this episode of my life into His plan for my life.

CHAPTER 15

STARTING TO DO THE TIME

S entencing day came when I was to report to the judge. To spare my family from witnessing that ordeal, we said our goodbyes at home, and I drove myself in.

Based on previous meetings and conversations, I thought we would convene in the judge's chambers where we had previously met. I was under my own false impression that I'd be driven over to the jail by a deputy who would let me sit up front with him and run through a fast food restaurant to get breakfast before dropping me off at the nice new dorm-like facility that I had heard about. WRONG!

Before I tell you what happened, let me first inform you that when our Heavenly Father says "Trust me," brace yourself for the unexpected situation that will produce visible evidence of the level of your confidence. You will not be able to "fake" it. Either you do, or you don't! Game playing is over!

Well, that morning I didn't ride up front with the deputy, and we didn't pick up breakfast at a fast-food restaurant. I didn't go to the judge's chambers. I walked into a packed courtroom. After being sentenced, I was handcuffed and placed in a concrete holding cell packed with several other men before being transferred to the county jail in a cramped van. We didn't go to the nice new dorm facility. We went to the old condemned jail, called Castle Gray-skull. As I was being led down the concrete corridor to my cell block the words, "Father, have you forgot about me," was starting to enter my conscious mind and becoming the forefront of my thoughts.

After going through several steel doors, I got to my cell block. My cell was on the second floor, and as I was walking up the steps, I looked over it into the TV area and saw a group of guys that looked as mean and evil as someone could look! I wondered if they knew cannibalism was against the law or even cared! As I sat down on my steel bunk with the thin one-inch mattress, my head was spinning and my heart pounding. I can't adequately describe my feeling of shock and disbelief. Everything that I had thought, professed, believed, and had spoken had been rocked to the core by that morning's events. After sitting there for a few minutes, I concluded that this had to be a mistake.

I started to get up to go call my wife. Something stopped me. I couldn't get up. It felt like someone had placed their hand on my shoulder, but there was no one in the cell. I realized that my Heavenly Father had checked me. With a whisper to my soul, He said, "Do you trust me?" I was bewildered! I realized that this was a defining moment where I had to determine whether

He was either my God of everything or God of nothing! I knew my response to these four words would forever change my life. I knew this was a time when I had to prove that I trusted him with my actions. I said, "Father, I'm sorry for doubting you because things haven't started as I thought. I choose to make you God of everything!" I also had to show a tangible demonstration of trusting my situation to His sovereign control. I had to realize there was no mistake. I was in my assigned seat, and I needed to embrace it as my task at hand.

As I stated earlier, did He cause this to happen? No one knows but Him. The only important factor at that point was that I trusted Him one hundred percent regardless of my thoughts, feelings, or conclusions. After pulling myself together, I walked out of my cell and noticed the guy in the next cell had an old paperback Bible. I asked him if I could borrow it and I took it back into my cell, sat down on my bunk and started reading.

A few minutes later he came into my cell, sat down, and started pouring out his soul. He shared that he was about to lose it all... his family, business, and kids. He didn't know where to turn. I got to share with him that our Heavenly Father loves him, has plans to prosper him and not to harm him, and is waiting to talk to him. I remember when he walked out of my cell, I humbly closed my eyes and thanked my Father for giving me the words to speak.

Within just a few minutes a second guy came into my cell, who I had never met. He began telling me his major life issues, and I got to share our Heavenly Father with him. A little later, a third guy came into my cell. He asked me if my accountant's office was at a particular location and if I knew the receptionist. I said yes. He told me that the receptionist was his mom. He said his mom had asked him if I was in with him. If so, I'd be someone for him to talk with. He was another one that was distraught, broken and feeling that all was lost. I got to share the good news of Jesus Christ with him as well.

Talk about timing - I had not spoken to the accountant's office in over a year. As to my knowledge, they had no idea as to the outcome, sentencing date, or where I would even be. The jail houses over 1600 people in two different buildings, on numerous floors with several pods on each floor. For me to end up in the same small pod as him – at that time – demonstrates the precise involvement of our Heavenly Father in our life!

When he left, I laid down on my bunk, turned my head to the wall and wept. I was totally overwhelmed at how my Heavenly Father had placed me with pinpoint accuracy in that cellblock - at that time in history - to bring the good news to three guys who felt that all was lost and had no hope for the future.

Another amazing part of this story to me is that just minutes before the first guy had entered my cell, I was the one distraught and having my world rocked. The only thing I did that changed me from being shaken to the core to being the one guiding them to hope was choosing to make Him first in my life, above everything. It's the same for you! You must turn control over to HIM and trust with child-like faith. He has you!

Later I was moved over to the new dorm facility, but I'll never forget the feeling I had as I walked down the long dark corridor to leave the first building. I left with total confidence that I had done everything that my Heavenly Father had sent me to do and that is the absolute best feeling in the world!

A few days later I was transferred to the state prison reception center where they evaluate and assign the facility where you will serve your sentence. During the orientation process, I met a guy who shared his story with me on why he had become an atheist. He told me that his dad died when he was 6. His mom not being financially able to take care of him took him to his grandparents and left him. She went to work in another state and would call him periodically and tell him that when she got financially able she would come get him. Years went by and one day she called and told him that she was coming to pick him up. He was so excited. She lived in Tennessee and was leaving that evening after she got off from work. He sat up most of the night waiting on her and about 3:00am they got a call from an Alabama state trooper notifying them that she had been killed in an automobile accident. He said that's when he became an atheist. He started believing that there was no such thing as a God because how could a loving God do that to him. With tears in my eyes, I said, "I don't know. I don't have specific answers, but I do know this one thing to be an absolute fact: you have a Heavenly Father. He loves you very much and wants to talk with you." We spent quite a bit of time daily talking about the benefits of letting God control your steps. He got transferred to another dorm and the only time I saw him again was in a chapel service the following week. It was amazing to see the difference that had occurred in his life in that one week. To God be all the glory!

A few days later, I was transferred to the main facility in another city. The minimum security work camp where I was assigned to be was next door. While I was at the main unit, one of the first guys I met was a paralytic whose bunk was a few rows down from mine. I learned that he got injured in a motorcycle accident while escaping from the police. He was a top-ranking member of a nationally known bad gang with a life sentence. His tattoos proved his activities required to get to his level, which he proudly displayed. Upon that discovery, I sure was thankful that he appeared to like the food I had shared with him!

On Friday we stayed up and talked - mostly about his life. He talked about his kids, crimes, the harbored hatred towards family and friends. He was extremely bitter. His ex-wife had told his kids that he was dead and had put an urn on the fireplace mantle that supposedly contained his ashes. His dad was a judge and his mom was also a high ranking government official. They had both disowned him. I sat and listened to him in absolute silence. I didn't even know what to say to respond. It was stories of meanness, cruelty, and hate in such levels that I couldn't comprehend existed, being told through staring eyes that reinforced their authenticity. The next day I attended chapel and during worship I asked the Heavenly Father what He would have me say. Before I even finished my question, while the thoughts were still in my mind and the words on my lips, He said, "Tell him the same thing I've told you to tell the others. Tell him I love him."

So Saturday night, the paralytic gang member and I talked again. He talked about his youngest daughter. I asked him if he could have anything in the world, what it would be. Without hesitation he said, "My kids. I want to see my little girl! I love her a lot!" I said you know that feeling you have that you call love? That comes from our Heavenly Father that loves you like you love your little girl. Actually, he's the one that gave you the ability to love her and he wants to talk to you. He has plans for your life... a plan to prosper you and not harm you. I know you feel all is lost but it's not. He said you don't know my family. They disowned me - nobody cares - nobody loves me.

I said no, I don't but our Heavenly Father knows them and He can do more in a split second that you and I can in a lifetime. Just talk to Him tonight when you go back to your bunk. Will you do that? He said yes. The next morning I talk with him about writing his mom and telling her he was sorry for the things he had done and asking her for forgiveness. Again he resisted and said, "No way. You don't know my mom." I said our Heavenly Father does and this is where it has to start. It has to begin with you manning up and saying, "I'm sorry."

The day after we talked, I got assigned my first job as an aid pushing a person in a wheelchair. Guess who I was assigned to? You guessed it – him! As our conversations continued, I surmised that he hadn't talk to the Heavenly Father, nor did he believe anything could change. At the end of the week, I was notified that I was being transferred to the minimum security camp next-door. So with our time together being short I felt I had to talk with him as much as possible since we only had a few days left and I knew I would probably never see him again. So my final night I challenged him as hard as I could. After I had heard all his excuses I said, "Let's face it. You're not man enough. Even in here with your ranking over other gang members, you're powerful and can hurt & kill people, but you're not man enough to pick up the phone, or pick up a pen and say, "Mom. I'm sorry." He became defiant, but he knew I was right. I knew he could have me taken out that night while I was asleep, but it didn't seem to matter. At that moment my attitude and words were - take me out and I'll be talking to Jesus about you - don't take me out and I'll be talking to you about Jesus. It was one of those

moments that I look back on now and say to myself, "What in the world was I thinking...?!?!"
The next morning as I was leaving, I told him that I would be praying for him. I wanted so bad to be able to spend more time with him but the Heavenly Father impressed upon me that He would take it from there. That was the last time I got to see him.

Over the next 30 months, until I was released, I seemed to be strategically placed by our Heavenly Father in numerous situations where I could share the story of His love. Also, our Heavenly Father continued to show me favoritism by giving me the most desirable bunk locations, best jobs and the most respectable dorm officers. Believe me, it's one of those experiences that I wish I would have never had to go through. But, at the same time, I wouldn't take anything for the journey.

Let's get back to the principles that certainly guided and enhanced my experience and can have an incredible impact on your life.

CHAPTER 16
SPIRIT OF EXCELLENCE

As it is stated throughout the Bible, first-fruit is the activator of our Heavenly Father's blessing. He says that if we do not rob Him of our first-fruit (tithes), He will pour out a blessing that will max our capacity, but He will only give access to the amount we can handle. Our blessing is to be for our good, not harm. After we activate the blessing on our life through first-fruit, there is an expected way we are to operate. Our level of performance is to elevate to the point of us putting forth the best effort we can. His blessing and sloppiness from us do not go together! Combining these two things would only serve as an insult to our Heavenly Father.

Since our blessing contains inexhaustible provisions, it behooves us to operate in a manner that will help us reach our full potential. It's expected of us. The Bible says that we work for our Heavenly Father no matter what job, position, or task He may have assigned us to (Colossians 3:23). Therefore, in His eyes, our vocation – (i.e., Truck Driver, Secretary, Doctor, Business Owner) is our service to Him. Since He expects the best with our worship, then it only makes sense that He would expect the best from our work, right?

When we think of our work from this aspect, it will make Monday as important as Sunday regarding honoring Him. Therefore, if He expects first-fruit, which signifies the best, then it only makes sense that He would expect the best from our work performance, right?

With your present position and work, you may feel that you've been neglected – treated unfairly – have the attitude that opportunity for success and promotions have passed you by, but that's when you view it in the natural. When you look at it from a spiritual standpoint that we work for our Heavenly Father, you understand that God has you, cares about you and will promote you when He knows you're ready – not when you think you are. He wants to give you good things. He wants you to have the best. He would love to give you the best at the company where you work, but we must be ready for the assignment.
When you grasp this, no matter what job He has you presently assigned to, your attitude, motivation, dedication, and appreciation will elevate. (Colossians 3:22, Ephesians 6:5, 1Timothy 6:1). He wants to give you the desires of your heart (Psalms 37:4).

Think about David and Joseph from the Bible - David catapulted from the pasture to the palace in one day. Joseph went from prison to the palace in one day. How can this happen? It's through promotions from our Heavenly Father, and the same principles that catapulted them can do it for you. It comes from operating with a Spirit of Excellence. David would

71

never have been used to kill Goliath if he had not honed his sheep protection skills while on the backside of the mountain. And if he had not killed Goliath, he would not have been promoted to the palace.

As Ron Carpenter, Senior Pastor of Redemption, said, "You have the potential for Greatness, but you don't have the knowledge for Greatness." Even though he had God's blessing, he would have never risen past tending the sheep if he had not applied his best effort to whatever he was doing. After Samuel came to Jesse's house and anointed David with oil, as God had instructed him to do, David went back to the field doing the same tiring, mundane chores of tending to the sheep (1 Samuel 16:12,19). But a little later, David went from obscurity to notoriety. He went from the bottom to the top – bypassing all the conventional procedures because he operated with a Spirit of Excellence when he was out on the back side of the mountain tending to the sheep! This is how God promotions are activated. David could've been disgruntled and discouraged when he compared himself to his brothers who had admired and prestigious positions in the army. He could've spent his time kicking rocks, instead of using the stones to develop a skill that would propel him to advancement in career, income, status, and influence. He used his time wisely and so should you!

No matter how you may be feeling now, don't let the present situation or your past define you – view it only as a time of preparation! God doesn't erase your future because of your past! Your reputation doesn't have to be your legacy. You're not defined by your mistakes. You're defined by our Heavenly Father. The enemy thought he had me, that the ordeal I'd been through would cause me to feel disappointed, inferior, or worthless.

According to man's label:

> They say – I have a Dept. of Corrections ID
> *God says* – I have a mandate
> They say – I'm an ex-con
> *God says* – I'm a chosen vessel
> They say – I've got a past
> *God says* – I've got a present and a future
> They say – My value has been diminished
> *God says* – I'm fearfully and wonderfully made
> They say – I have limited possibilities
> *God says* – He has a plan to prosper me and give me the desires of my heart, that's exceedingly, abundantly above all that I could ask or think.
> They say – I can't get a job at the food court.
> *God says* – He doesn't want me supersizing fries! He wants me supersizing the motivation of people that are hurting to boost their faith, confidence, and commitment to the level that will cause them to change the direction of their life!

Don't let anything stop you from being all that God wants you to be! He doesn't bring condemnation or

73

disqualification or revoke His plan for you because of a mistake (Romans 11:29). He brings Mercy and Grace to you, proving that your present situation can be summed up in one word – TEMPORARY!
(2 Corinthians 4:18)

It's hard for us to fully grasp Mercy and Grace because it is so far beyond our ability to comprehend. Mercy is not getting what we deserve, and Grace is getting what we don't deserve. Let me give you an illustration. Let's say you are before a Judge who is about to sentence you for a heinous crime. You're expecting to go to prison for the rest of your life. But, the judge says, "I'm not going to sentence you to any time. I'm dropping the charge against you. You're free to go." That's Mercy - not getting what we deserve! Now, in addition to letting you go free, let's say the Judge also gave you fifty thousand dollars." That's Grace - getting what we don't deserve! It's hard to believe that scenario would happen. But, it's harder for us to attempt to understand His Mercy and Grace!

While our Heavenly Father is waiting for you to prepare for elevation, you feel as if you are in a similar situation to David when he was a shepherd. But instead of honing, nurturing, and developing your skills, you are too absorbed in your self-evaluation that permeates the idea that you have been looked over, jumped over, scooted over, knocked over and on a dead-end street. But look at it from a different perspective. Look at it with the understanding that –

#1 – Our Heavenly Father is your employer, and He's the one that handles all positions and promotions.

#2 – Since He wants to prosper you, then maybe you're where you are so you can develop the skill set required for your next assignment.

Perhaps you need to develop your work ethic to the level of operating with a spirit of excellence where you do the absolute best job you can do in everything you do so He will be pleased with what you do.

If your work ethic and dedication to excellence pleases our Heavenly Father, believe me, your boss will love it. Promotions and raises will become customary. But, if your work attitude is to do just enough not to get fired, you will NEVER get a break! David probably thought that his skills were only necessary to fulfill his present occupation. He didn't know that what was actually happening was that God was going to take him beyond anything he could ever dream. I can visualize our Heavenly Father smiling as David was taking his brothers something to eat. He knew that David had no idea that he was about to become one of the most influential men of his day and for the rest of history. On that day, it was impossible for David to believe it. The next day, it was impossible for him not to believe.

But, if David had not operated with a spirit of excellence while on the back side of the mountain, he would not have honed his skills to match his future assignment of killing Goliath - even though he had NO idea what it was. He would have simply dropped off lunch and returned to the backside of the mountain and would NEVER have fulfilled his assignment for that day and altering his future forever!

It's the same way with you. You have no idea what God has planned for you and how he wants to use you. Don't get so busy feeling messed over, but concentrate on developing your skills so you'll be prepared and capable for your next assignment. You must be ready. Your skillset and mindset must be capable of the task.

BLOWING THE LEAVES - A FRIEND'S REAL LIFE STORY OF EXCELLENCE

A friend of mine was a builder who had gone through some tough times financially. On the way, home one day, he noticed leaves piling up on the roof of a house from a big overhanging oak tree. He stopped and offered to blow the leaves off the roof for twenty-five dollars. Unfortunately, neither he nor the homeowner had a leaf blower. He went to his house and connected an electrical cord to a squirrel cage blower and used it. It blew leaves everywhere, and even though it wasn't part of the deal, he said he felt bad about the leaves being all over the yard, so he raked the leaves into a pile. As he was getting paid, he told the owner that he needed to make a few bucks and asked if there was anything else that he would like to have done. The owner was impressed with him going beyond what he was obligated to do (we call that operating with the Spirit of Excellence, right?) that he kept him doing one project after another. When he finished the various jobs, he was paid over sixteen thousand dollars, developed a tremendously satisfied customer and referral source that produced more work than he could do alone. He had to hire two crews to help him keep up with all the business.

That's how our Heavenly Father rewards excellence! You have no idea of the people He has lined up for you to meet or the direction He has for you to go. You have no idea what He has lined up for you to accomplish. And right now, it may be hard for you to believe what I'm saying, but by this time next week or next month, it could be impossible for you not to believe. Remember, you are a child of our Heavenly Father with a specific purpose and unlimited resources to fulfill your purpose!

By the way – here is another personal example of His favor I received by operating under the First-fruit blessing with a continued Spirit of Excellence. When I arrived at the Work-Release Center for the last six months of my sentence, we all had to find work and provide for our own transportation. Most rode a $10 bike in the cold rain to and from a less-than-desired job. The favor I received put me in a fantastic job that included being picked in a new F250 truck with a Starbucks on the console.

Bottom line - there's no denying His blessing.

Following His system is the key that yields success.
Nothing is better than having His favor!

Chapter 17

Develop A Friendship With Him

Our Heavenly Father has been eagerly awaiting you to come home. Jesus demonstrates this perfectly in the parable of the Lost Son. The story is about a young man who asked his father for his part of the family inheritance. He left home and wasted his money in wild living.

Now he's broke, and he began to starve. He got a job feeding pigs and became so hungry that he started to eat their food. But then he came to his senses and thought about how the servants of his father ate much better than this.

He decided to go back home and ask his father if he could just be a servant. He rehearsed the speech for his dad and took off toward home. While he was still a long way off, his father saw him coming. Filled with love and compassion, he ran to his son, embraced him, and kissed him. His son said to him, "Father, I have sinned against both heaven and you, and I am no longer worthy of being called your son." But his father said to the servants, 'Quick! Bring the finest robe in the house and put it on him. Get a ring for his finger and sandals for his feet. And kill the calf we have been fattening. We must celebrate with a feast, for this son of mine was dead and has now returned to life. He was lost, but now he is found." Luke 15:21-24 (NLT).

That's exactly how He feels toward you – He's been looking for you to come home. Once you turn toward Him, He's going to run to you – hug you – and love on you. Then He'll get you doing what He planned for you when he made you.

Know this - You are ACCEPTED!

Talk to Him just as if you were talking to your best friend – because He is! Ask Him what He wants you to do and ask Him to help you. You have so much potential, but He will not violate Free Will. It's your choice. And remember, you're only effective when you're authentic.

As I began spending time with Him in the mornings before anything else (first-fruit time), it was as if I could hear Him saying that He wanted to give me the desires of my heart and asking me, "What do you want to do?"

Don't feel inadequate about doing anything He leads you to do. Just always do your best wherever He puts you. If you focus on Him, abide by the principle of first-fruit, and operate with a Spirit of Excellence, He will orchestrate the circumstances. What university did Abraham attend to learn how to make his livestock reproduce, increase and multiply so rapidly – so much so that he and Lot had to separate due to the land not being able to support their cattle? (Genesis 13) Where did Isaac hear it? Jacob? At what university did Solomon acquire all his knowledge?

Ray Crock was 54
Colonel Sanders was 65

Don't worry if the time is right to do what you feel led to do. Ray Crock was 54 when he started McDonald's. Colonel Sanders was 65 when he started KFC. Jentezen Franklin, the Senior Pastor of Free Chapel Worship Center, said, "The Colonel spent two years driving around the country with chicken recipes that were turned down 1009 times." So, don't worry about being too old or too "anything," just start going toward it! I'm writing this book at the age of 60!

CHAPTER 18

SUCCESSFUL BUT NOT SATISFIED

Actor Jim Carrey said, "I wish people could realize all their dreams of wealth and fame, so that they could see it's not where you are going to find your sense of completion." What a powerful statement! You may find yourself in a situation where you are doing well financially, but not feeling inwardly satisfied. If financial success and material possessions brought a feeling of significance, Hollywood would be the most delightful city in America. These were never designed to satisfy unless used for their legitimate purpose. Material blessings are to be enjoyed and used for the advancement of His kingdom, not for a self-centered living (1 Tim 6:17-18).

We are sent to earth at a precise time, a particular location, with access to full resources, and a certain amount of allotted days to accomplish our mission before our deadline. Think of it like a soldier sent on a mission. You want a feeling of incredible significance? Use His resources for your intended assignment, which involves balance. "Of course, I don't mean your giving should make life easy for others and hard for yourselves. I only mean that there should be some equality." (2 Corinthians 8:13 NLT) The finality aspect of our existence on earth should intensify our efforts toward accomplishing our personal mission. Everything else in our life is temporary. The mere fact that the accomplishment of our mission is the only thing we will be rewarded for should create within us a real sense of urgency! These are the only things we truly own that last forever and are at the forefront of the mind of Jesus. He said, "Look, I am coming soon, bringing my reward with me to repay all people according to their deeds." (Revelation 22:12 NLT) Our Heavenly Father has given you the intelligence, resources, and abilities you possess to make a greater impact on your life. When used to seize the opportunities - He orchestrates in your life, the harvest is much more than you can imagine. Let this be a moment of discovery. Get serious about discovering your dream and pursuing your purpose that will... Max Your Talents! Make the appropriate assessments and determinations you need to make. As stated in a previous chapter, dreams will demand integrity and discipline. If you really want to change, you can! It will take commitment! But, nothing can stop you if you make the determination to do it!

BURN THE SHIP - A FRIEND'S REAL LIFE STORY OF COMMITMENT

Let me give you a real-life story of what total commitment looks like. Some time back a friend was getting a divorce. It had been a very long and painful ordeal, but the time had come for them to meet at the lawyer's office the next morning to sign the final divorce papers. The night before, my friend started reading a book about Captain Hernán Cortés when he landed in Veracruz to begin his great conquest in 1519. Upon arriving, he gave the order to his men to burn the ships. He knew that the chance of victory was extremely slim for his small group of men. Cortés was on a mission, and he was aware that the only way to keep himself or his men from quitting on the mission was to take that option off the table. What Cortés did was force himself and his men to either win or die.

My friend said the story resonated with him. Something happened on the inside. He woke up the next morning and went to the lawyer's office. As he burst through the door, he said, "I know we're here to sign papers, but I didn't come to sign." He tells them the story from the book and says, "I'm burning the ship! I'm not signing divorce papers, and I'm coming home tonight! I'll carry you to dinner or cook your dinner, you make a choice! I made a commitment to be here, and I'm going to be here." He rips up the papers and that evening he went back home!

That was a few years back, and today they are still together. I believe it's one hundred percent attributed to his commitment, and the rewards are visibly blossoming in all areas of his life. His marriage is doing great! His wife is doing great! His kids are doing great, and his business is doing great. Recently, I heard that he made more money on one deal than most Americans make in a lifetime!

And that's just one of the many deals that are pouring in. Remember the earlier notes about Obed-Edom's house when God blessed him. It stated that his whole household came under intensive blessing. He, his family, and everything around him were blessed! I believe wholeheartedly that if my friend had not made the commitment to do the right thing back then, he would not be enjoying the season of success he's enjoying today... the harvest that comes from making a commitment and operating with a Spirit of Excellence!

Make a total commitment and Burn the ship!

Everybody would like to be him now, but how many would have made the commitment and lived with the unknown circumstances for the years it took to get to where he is now! You want his kind of results? Do his kind of things! Take a stand! Make a total commitment and "Burn the ship!"

This story was a real-life story – showing the marvelous dynamics that can emerge from a total commitment! The following "Mercedes" story is my personal experience that illustrates how important it is to make sure that you place value on the right things.

MY MERCEDES STORY – MY PERSONAL STORY ABOUT THINGS OF IMPORTANCE

Some years ago, I bought my dream car - a Mercedes S500. I remember driving back from the dealership in Georgia. What a feeling! I was so thrilled. I remember when the first bug hit the windshield on I-85. I wanted to stop and clean it. For the first few months, I would drive it only in beautiful weather. No one could eat in the car. It was always clean. It was my showcase!

Six months down the road, conditions had changed. I drove in the rain, it would get dirty, and kids could eat in it. One day as I was leaving work, my wife asked me to pick up a gallon of milk. I stopped at the convenience store, and as I started into the store, I heard someone say, "That's my baby. That's my dream!" I turned and saw a man standing in front of the car. I then looked at the car, and my thoughts went back to the day I had driven it home. What a thrill. I thought about how I had treated it originally. How it was a prized possession with special conditions for use. But six months later it was just another vehicle to drive to pick up a gallon of milk. I looked back over at the man, paused for a second, then said, "Dream Bigger!"

As I continued into the store, I couldn't help but think about how something that seemed so important a few months earlier now seemed so average, ordinary, and insignificant. After that encounter, I began to ponder quite often about how many other things was I giving temporary cherishment to that in some short period of time would fall into the category of ill-guided value.

What's your "Mercedes"?

Have you had a similar incident or thought? What's

the "Mercedes" in your life? What seems so important to you now? House - car - boat - business - position? Whatever it is, at some time in the future you'll look back, and it's going to have lost its "significant" value if it's not something that helps you positively impact the lives of others and further the Kingdom of God. However, if you will focus your intelligence, resources, and opportunities in the right direction, you will be overwhelmed with a feeling of worth, and nothing you do will end up in the irrelevant category!

Chapter 19
Start Immediately!

Regardless of how you got to the place in your life where you are now, the important question is what are you going to do now?

There's a series of steps that have brought you to where you are, and there will be a series of steps that will take you out of where you are. It's not by magic, it's by the process. Understand that the enemy's main tactic is PROCRASTINATION! Be aware of his efforts to get you to Procrastinate – to put off starting. He doesn't mind how excited you get about what you're capable of achieving as long as you start... *tomorrow!* Don't let the enemy paralyze you! Your progress is not hindered by your environment. Jim Rohn said, "Without a sense of urgency, desire loses its value."

Keep a sense of urgency and start:

> Giving First-fruit
> Operating with Excellence
> Developing a Friendship with your Heavenly Father
> Sharing YOUR Story

Also, write down the thing(s) that interests you. As you

begin to meditate on what interests you, ideas, and thoughts about how to put these into action will start popping into your head. You'll start developing a passion, which is your motivation! Your passion is what sets fire to your purpose. Ferdinand Foch said, "The most powerful weapon on earth is the human soul on fire!"

As you become passionate, your initial thoughts and ideas have now begun to resonate inside of you to the level that it has now become your dream! At this point, pursue your passion with persistence, prayer, and commitment! Your ideas have consequences. You start visualizing how exciting it would be to see this come to fruition. As you go from your initial ideas to the dream stage, you may start wondering if this is God's purpose for you. To explore this, Rev. Jack Graham, PowerPoint Ministries, recommends asking yourself the following questions:

> Is my dream consistent with scripture?
> Does it conform to the law of Love?
> Does it bless people?
> Do I continually give thanks to our Heavenly Father for it?
> Is it confirmed by Godly counsel?
> Does it call me to a greater dependency and obedience to our Heavenly Father?
> If you answer "yes" to these questions, then proceed with confidence that you are on the right track in pursuing our Heavenly Father's purpose for your life.

And as you start putting your thoughts and ideas into action, always remember: Understand your uniqueness – nobody is like you! If our Heavenly Father gives you a dream, nothing can stop you – but you! Your calling is always a benefit to Kingdom expansion! He will not reveal your purpose past your commitment! Our Heavenly Father must always be first!

Your purpose may be behind the scenes. My wife's passion is giving to the needy. For years, she has gotten a large store to donate their damaged bent-can food and opened clothing, which she gives to the group that distributes to the needy. She loves to do this and considers it to be her purpose. It is very much needed and is done behind the scene. If she were asked to speak in front of a group, she would probably die.

The point being that you don't have to be up front to be effective. We all have a part to play, and your part will be what you are passionate about doing.
In the InTouch publication, Ginger Garrett wrote an article that stated, "Our role in the kingdom body may be so essential that it simply goes unnoticed. We may know our heart is beating, or that air is going in and out of our lungs, but the cilia inside the intestines that absorb vitamins from food may be making this essential function without acknowledgment." No matter if our service is something seen by man, or not, doing what God has purposed us to do is all that counts.

I have a friend who's been actively involved in the Big

Brothers/Big Sisters program for years. She has been the "Big Sister" since her first girl was very young. That girl has now graduated from college. Even though they are still connected – my friend became the Big Sister of another little girl. In addition to the second girl, she recently added a third girl. What a great accomplishment to make a positive impact on the lives of these little girls. But, she's not only connected with Big Brothers/Big Sisters, she is also involved with a group who feed the homeless. These years of passionate service validates her passion and purpose as she pushes toward her purpose.

I have another close friend who has been actively involved in Teen Challenge for years. He not only teaches a class at the facility each week but has taken an active part in daily mentoring, employment, as well as providing a place to live and transportation to many of these guys who are battling drug addiction and other life issues.

I feel one of his greatest accomplishments is how he has instilled the outreach mindset into his son, who has been featured in both newspaper and publication articles for his benevolent activities. But it doesn't stop there. He has started passing it down to his son and what's remarkable is that he began when his son was only four years old.

As Derrick Brooks was being inducted into the Football Hall of Fame, he said, "The NFL allowed me a stage, but I tell people all the time: You don't have to be a football player to make a difference. All you need is time and a willing heart. If you give your time, you can change the world." Becoming involved starts kindling your passion - leads to action - and creates commitment. If your passion is teaching youth to play a sport, start now to find a coach you can help and grow from there.

Start sharing your story and watch everything develop from there! Maybe you've overcome a traumatic experience in your life, such as beating cancer or some other dreaded disease. Now that you know how it feels to be told bad news by your doctor, you feel passionate to share your story with someone that's facing the same thing. Find a person experiencing the same thing and share your story. If it's spousal abuse, find someone going through it. Whatever it may be that you've been through, find someone going through it and start sharing your story!

It will be so subtle, and if you aren't aware of it, you will even agree with it. But it yields the most disastrous outcome in your life. The enemy uses three words to make up a vicious and powerfully effective lie: Plenty of time! The enemy doesn't care what you plan to accomplish as long as you start tomorrow. He knows you are going to be energized and feeling empowered after reading this book. Count on with certainty that he will try to deflate you. One of the main ways is through procrastination. If you put off starting until tomorrow, he wins! So, don't put it off. In 2 Corinthians 2:10-12, it states for us not to be ignorant of the enemy's devices.

Be careful! One of the enemy's most effective Plenty-of-Time procrastination strategies is simply to use our routine of life! He knows if we don't start NOW, our motivation will decline to the point where it's back to our daily routine and before we know it, another week, month, or year is gone!

CLIMBING ACCIDENT - A FRIEND'S REAL LIFE STORY ABOUT ATTITUDE

One of my best friends was a great athlete, super student, loved by everyone, and had so much potential. He had a mountain climbing accident that left him paralyzed when he was 15 years old. It was an awful tragedy in every sense of the word. Even though the ordeal could have left him extremely bitter, he didn't allow it. No matter what he had to endure, he kept a positive attitude. He didn't let his physical condition stop him from doing what he wanted to do. Over the last 25 years, as a paraplegic, I've seen him snow ski, snowmobile, jet ski, sail, parachute, participate in the New York Marathon, along with numerous triathlons and bike races. During this time he also became one of the Top-Rated Tennis players in the world... but he could never beat me - LOL! These are just a few of his many achievements.
Some time back a person asked him how he could stay so positive and not get discouraged with all he had been through. His quick reply was simply, "I don't go there!" I'm saying the same thing to you - DON'T GO THERE! Don't think about your past. Don't think about your failures or what you wish you could do-over. Think about your future and GO THERE! !

CHAPTER 20
PERSONAL NOTE TO YOU!

No matter how you got this book, our Heavenly Father knew before He formed the world that you would be reading it right now - at this given time! Amazing, isn't it? Remember back at the beginning of the book I told you how valuable you were to Him? This is just another instance of proof.

You would smile if you had a glimpse of the marvelous converging of circumstances and orchestrated events He arranged for you to get this book. You got it ~ you read it – now apply it and experience your life change! Let our Heavenly Father start leading you in the fulfilling life He planned for you!

I would love to hear from you! **I want to hear your story.** I would also like to help you discover your OWN uniqueness, as well as assisting you in getting focused on finding and fulfilling your purpose!

Please go to our website and register so we can connect at: www.JoinWithDestiny.com

I look forward to hearing from you,

Gary Calhoun

FIRST-FRUIT SCRIPTURES

There are many scriptures that validate our Heavenly Father's attitude and instructions for giving and the importance He places on first-fruit. Here are a few.

Exodus 23:16,19: "Second, celebrate the Festival of Harvest, when you bring me the first crops of your harvest." "As you harvest your crops, bring the very best of the first harvest to the house of the Lord your God."

Nehemiah 10:37: We will store the produce in the storerooms of the Temple of our God. We will bring the best of our flour and other grain offerings, the best of our fruit, and the best of our new wine and olive oil. And we promise to bring to the Levites a tenth of everything our land produces, for it is the Levites who collect the tithes in all our rural towns.

Proverbs 3:8-10 (NKJV): Honor the Lord with your possessions and with the first-fruits of all your increase; so, your barns will be filled with plenty, and your vats will overflow with new wine.

Ezekiel 44:30 (NKJV): The best of all first-fruits of any

kind, and every sacrifice of any kind from all your sacrifices, shall be the priest's; also, you shall give to the priest the first of your ground meal, to cause a blessing to rest on your house.

Leviticus 2:12 (NKJV): As for the offering of the First-fruits, you shall offer them to the Lord, but they shall not be burned on the altar for a sweet aroma.

Leviticus 27:30: "One-tenth of the produce of the land, whether grain from the fields or fruit from the trees, belongs to the Lord and must be set apart to him as holy."

Deuteronomy 18:4 (NKJV): The first-fruits of your grain and your new wine and your oil, and the first of the fleece of your sheep, you shall give him.

1 Corinthians 15:20-23: But in fact, Christ has been raised from the dead. He is the first of a great harvest of all who have died.

Matthew 22:21 (NKJV): They said to Him, "Caesar's." And He said to them, "Render therefore to Caesar the things that are Caesar's, and to God the things that are God's."

Brian Zahnd wrote a book about it titled, "What to do on the worst day of your life." It's a powerful book that I recommend reading! It tells the story of David and his men coming home to Ziklag after a battle only to find their homes burned down, their possessions stolen, and their families taken captive. It was the worst day of David's life. It's a great example of what to do and it is based on what David did found in I Samuel, Chapter 30.

What areas did Max Your Talents help you the most?

_____

_____

_____

_____

_____

_____

_____

_____

_____

_____

_____

_____

Write down your daily struggles and how you can respond more effectively?

_____

_____

_____

_____

_____

_____

_____

_____

_____

_____

_____

_____

What's Your Dream?

_____

_____

_____

_____

_____

_____

If you are ready to pursue your Dream, what do you need to do first?

_____

_____

_____

_____

What personal areas do you need to improve to operate with a Spirit of Excellence?

_____

_____

_____

_____

_____

_____

_____

_____

_____

_____

_____

_____

Notes

Notes

Be sure to register at:
www.JoinWithDestiny.com

Notes

CPSIA information can be obtained
at www.ICGtesting.com
Printed in the USA
LVOW12s0320101117
555747LV00003B/235/P